Domestic Work

Domestic Work

POEMS BY

Natasha Trethewey

Winner of the 1999 Cave Canem Poetry Prize

Selected and Introduced by Rita Dove

Graywolf Press
Saint Paul, Minnesota

Publication of this volume is made possible in part by a grant provided by the Minnesota State Arts Board through an appropriation by the Minnesota State Legislature, and by a grant from the National Endowment for the Arts. Significant support has also been provided by the Bush Foundation; Dayton's, Mervyn's, and Target stores through the Dayton Hudson Foundation; the McKnight Foundation; and other generous contributions from foundations, corporations, and individuals. To these organizations and individuals we offer our heartfelt thanks.

Additional funding for this title was provided by the Jerome Foundation.

Published by Graywolf Press
2402 University Avenue, Suite 203
Saint Paul, Minnesota 55114
All rights reserved.

www.graywolfpress.org

Published in the United States of America

ISBN 1-55597-309-4

2 4 6 8 9 7 5 3

Library of Congress Catalog Card Number: 00-101775

Cover art: Romare Bearden, *Evening Guitar* © Romare Bearden
Foundation/Licensed by VAGA, New York, NY

Cover design: Jeanne Lee

Acknowledgments

Thanks to the editors of the following journals in which these poems, sometimes in different versions, first appeared:

African American Review: "At the Owl Club, North Gulfport, Mississippi, 1950," "Gesture of a Woman in Process," "His Hands"

AGNI: "Drapery Factory, Gulfport, Mississippi,1956," "Naola Beauty Academy, New Orleans, 1943"

The American Poetry Review: "Amateur Fighter"

Callaloo: "Flounder," "Three Photographs," "Accounting," "Tableau," "Expectant," "Hot Combs," "Saturday Drive," "History Lesson," "Self-Employment"

Crazyhorse: "Cameo"

The Gettysburg Review: "Domestic Work, 1937"

Greensboro Review: "Speculation, 1939"

The Massachusetts Review: "Collection Day"

New England Review: "Limen"

New Virginia Review: "Mythmaker"

The North American Review: "Family Portrait"

Painted Bride Quarterly: "Saturday Matinee"

Poet Lore: "Early Evening, Frankfort, Kentucky," "Picture Gallery"

Seattle Review: "Give and Take," "White Lies," "Microscope"

Southern Humanities Review: "Gathering"

The Southern Review: "At the Station"

"Limen" also appeared in *The Best American Poetry 2000,* edited by Rita Dove and David Lehman, published by Scribner, 2000.

"Cameo" and "Naola Beauty Academy, New Orleans, 1943" also appeared in *The New Young American Poets,* edited by Kevin Prufer, published by Southern Illinois University Press, 2000.

"Collection Day" and "White Lies" also appeared in *Boomer Girls: Poems by Women of the Baby Boom Generation,* edited by Pamela Gemin and Paula Sergi, published by the University of Iowa Press, 1999.

"White Lies" also appeared in *Welcome to Your Life: Writings for the Heart of Young America,* edited by David Haynes and Julie Landsman, published by Milkweed Editions, 1998.

"Domestic Work, 1937," "Naola Beauty Academy, New Orleans, 1943," "Drapery Factory, Gulfport, Mississippi, 1956," "Collection Day," "Hot Combs," and "Secular" also appeared in *Spirit and Flame: An Anthology of African American Poetry,* edited by Keith Gilyard, published by Syracuse University Press, 1997.

"Flounder" and "White Lies" also appeared in *Two Worlds Walking: A Mixed-Blood Anthology,* edited by Diane Glancy and C.W. Truesdale, published by New Rivers Press, 1994.

"Drapery Factory, Gulfport, Mississippi, 1956" and "Naola Beauty Academy, New Orleans, 1943" also appeared in *On the Verge: Emerging Poets,* edited by Thomas Sayers Ellis and Joseph Lease, published by New Cambridge Press, 1994.

For My Father

Contents

IV

Introduction by Rita Dove

"People are trapped in history," James Baldwin has said, "and history is trapped in them." Natasha Trethewey takes up this double-edged sword and, like the fabled knights of yore, goes forth to engage the world. She identifies her mission early on, in a poem called "Three Photographs," whose last section describes a group of black laundresses:

> The eyes of eight women
> I don't know
> stare out from this photograph
> saying *remember*.

In the calm and unsmiling gaze of these women, one senses not an entreaty, but a challenge: to bear witness and give face to the legions of nameless men and women who cooked, scrubbed, welded, shoveled, hauled, and planted for an entire nation, helping to turn the American Dreamscape into reality.

Lest such a mission be considered too grand an undertaking for a poet, remember the words of Percy Bysshe Shelley, quintessential Romantic, who boldly claimed poets to be "the unacknowledged legislators of the world." The world of Natasha Trethewey's poetry is peopled with working-class African Americans. Although family members put in an appearance here and there, Trethewey resists the lure of autobiography and is careful to avoid such narrow identification, weaving no less than a tapestry of ancestors—farmhands and factory workers, hairdressers and stevedores, black men and women who built the future of their families and their race with their bare hands. With a steely grace reminiscent of those eight washerwomen, she tells the hard facts of lives pursued on the margins, lived out under oppression and in scripted oblivion, with fear and a tremulous hope. There's the work-at-home seamstress who wears a wig every day just in case someone drops by; an elevator operator who occupies her time looking for signs of fortune in every mole and palm-itch; the father turned amateur boxer who has learned to survive by "holding his body up to pain."

Trethewey eschews the Polaroid instant, choosing to render the unsuspecting yearnings and tremulous hopes that accompany our most private thoughts—reclaiming for us that interior life where the true self flourishes and to which we return, in solitary reverie, for strength. Just listen to the lilt and longing in this expectant mother's daydreaming:

> She can fill a room
>
> with a loud clear alto, broom-dance
> right out the back door, her heavy footsteps
>
> a parade beneath the stars.
>
> ["Expectant"]

From sonnets and traditional ballads to free verses shot through with the syncopated attitude of blues, the poems in *Domestic Work* sing with a muscular luminosity. Here is a young poet in full possession of her craft, ready to testify. To which I say: Can we get an "Amen?" And: Let these voices be heard.

I

Gesture of a Woman-in-Process

—from a photograph, 1902

In the foreground, two women,
their squinting faces
creased into texture—

a deep relief—the lines
like palms of hands
I could read if I could touch.

Around them, their dailiness:
clotheslines sagged with linens,
a patch of greens and yams,

buckets of peas for shelling.
One woman pauses for the picture.
The other won't be still.

Even now, her hands circling,
the white blur of her apron
still in motion.

At the Owl Club, North Gulfport, Mississippi, 1950

Nothing idle here—the men
so casual, each lean, each
tilted head and raised glass
a moment's stay from work.

Son Dixon's center of it all,
shouldering the cash register.
This is where his work is:
the New Orleans tailored suits,

shining keys, polished wood
and mirrors of the bar.
A white Cadillac out front.
Money in his pocket, a good cigar.

The men gather here after work,
a colored man's club. Supper
served in the back—gumbo, red beans,
talk of the Negro Leagues.

They repeat in leisure
what they've done all day—
stand around the docks, waiting
for a call, for anything to happen,

a chance to heave crates of bananas
and spiders. A risky job, its only
guarantee the consolation check
for a dead man's family.

Their lace-up boots say *shipyard*.
Dirt-caked trousers, *yard work*.
Regal Quarts in hand—
It's payday man.

Three Photographs

—by Clifton Johnson, 1902

1. Daybook, April 1901

What luck to find them here!
Through my lens, I watch them
strain against motion, hold still

for my shutter to open and close—
two Negro men, clothes like church,
collecting flowers in a wood,

pine needles and ivy twisting round.
I think to call it *Bouquets for Sweethearts,*
a blessing though their faces

hold little emotion. And yet,
they make such good subjects.
Always easy to pose,

their childlike curiosity.
How well this arbor frames
my shot—an intimate setting,

the boughs nestling us
like brothers. How fortunate still
to have found them here

instead of farther along
by that old cemetery
too full with new graves

and no flowers.

2. Cabbage Vendor

Natural, he say.
What he want from me?
Say he gone look through that hole—
his spirit box—
and watch me sell my cabbages
to make a picture hold
this moment, forever.
Nothing natural last
forever. When I'm in my garden
tearing these cabbages
from earth, hearing them scream
at the break, my fingers
brown as dirt—that's natural.
Or when I be in my kitchen
frying up salt pork
to cook that cabbage,
them meeting in the pot
like kin—that's natural.
Grown cabbage and cook cabbage
don't keep. Even dead
don't keep same.
But he will keep my picture,
unnatural like hoodoo love.
I could work a root of my own,
turn that thing around
and make him see himself
like he be seeing me—
distant and small—forever.

3. Wash Women

The eyes of eight women
I don't know
stare out from this photograph
saying *remember.*
Hung against these white walls,
their dark faces, common
as ones I've known,
stand out like some distant Monday
I've only heard about.
I picture wash day:
red beans simmering on the stove,
a number three tin tub
on the floor, well-water ready
to boil. There's cook-starch
for ironing, and some
left over to eat.

I hear the laughter,
three sisters speaking
of penny drinks, streetcars,
the movie house. A woman
like my grandmother rubs linens
against the washboard ribs,
hymns growing in her throat.
By the window, another
soaks crocheted lace, then presses
each delicate roll, long fingers
wet and glistening.
And in the doorway, the eldest

shifts her milk-heavy breasts,
a pile of strangers' clothes,
soiled, at her feet.

But in his photograph,
women do not smile,
their lips a steady line
connecting each quiet face.
They walk the road toward home,
a week's worth of take-in laundry
balanced on their heads
lightly as church hats. Shaded
by their loads, they do not squint,
their ready gaze through him,
to me, straight ahead.

II

Domestic Work

For Leretta Dixon Turnbough,
born June 22, 1916

I shirk not. I long for work. I pant for a life full of striving.
—W.E.B. DuBois

Domestic Work, 1937

All week she's cleaned
someone else's house,
stared down her own face
in the shine of copper-
bottomed pots, polished
wood, toilets she'd pull
the lid to—that look saying

Let's make a change, girl.

But Sunday mornings are hers—
church clothes starched
and hanging, a record spinning
on the console, the whole house
dancing. She raises the shades,
washes the rooms in light,
buckets of water, Octagon soap.

Cleanliness is next to godliness . . .

Windows and doors flung wide,
curtains two-stepping
forward and back, neck bones
bumping in the pot, a choir
of clothes clapping on the line.

Nearer my God to Thee . . .

She beats time on the rugs,
blows dust from the broom
like dandelion spores, each one
a wish for something better.

Speculation, 1939

First, the moles on each hand—
That's money by the pan—

and always the New Year's cabbage
and black-eyed peas. Now this,
another remembered adage,
her palms itching with promise,

she swears by the signs—*Money coming soon.*
But from where? Her left-eye twitch
says she'll see the boon.
Good—she's tired of the elevator switch,

those closed-in spaces, white men's
sideways stares. Nothing but
time to think, make plans
each time the doors slide shut.

What's to be gained from this New Deal?
Something finer like beauty school
or a milliner's shop—she loves the feel
of marcelled hair, felt and tulle,

not this all day standing around,
not that elevator lurching up, then down.

Secular

Workweek's end
and there's enough
block-ice in the box
to chill a washtub of colas
and one large melon,
dripping green.
After service, each house
opens heavy doors to street and woods,
one clear shot from front to back—
bullet, breeze, or holler.
A neighbor's *Yoo-hoo* reaches her
out back, lolling, pulling in wash,
pillow slips billowing
around her head like clouds.
Up the block,
a brand new graphanola,
parlor music, blues parlando—
Big Mama, Ma Rainey, Bessie—
Baby shake that thing like a saltshaker.
Lipstick, nylons
and she's out the door,
tipping past the church house,
Dixie Peach in her hair,
greased forehead shining
like gospel, like gold.

Signs, Oakvale, Mississippi, 1941

The first time she leaves home is with a man.
On Highway 49, heading North, she watches
the pine woods roll by, and counts on one hand
dead possum along the road, crows in splotches
of light—she knows to watch the signs for luck.
He has a fine car, she thinks. *And money green
enough to buy a dream*—more than she could tuck
under the mattress, in a Bible, or fold between
her powdered breasts. He'd promised land to farm
back home, new dresses, a house where she'd be
queen. (*Was that gap in his teeth cause for alarm?*)
The cards said *go.* She could roam the Delta, see
things she'd never seen. Outside her window,
nothing but cotton and road signs—*stop* or *slow*.

Expectant

Nights are hardest, the swelling,
tight and low (a girl), Delta heat,

and that woodsy silence a zephyred hush.
So how to keep busy? Wind the clocks,

measure out time to check the window,
or listen hard for his car on the road.

Small tasks done and undone, a floor
swept clean. She can fill a room

with a loud clear alto, broom-dance
right out the back door, her heavy footsteps

a parade beneath the stars. Honeysuckle
fragrant as perfume, nightlife

a steady insect hum. Still, she longs
for the Quarter—lights, riverboats churning,

the tinkle of ice in a slim bar glass.
Each night a refrain, its plain blue notes

carrying her, slightly swaying, home.

Tableau

At breakfast, the scent of lemons,
just-picked, yellowing on the sill.
At the table, a man and woman.

Between them, a still life:
shallow bowl, damask plums
in one square of morning light.

The woman sips tea
from a chipped blue cup, turning it,
avoiding the rough white edge.

The man, his thumb pushing deep
toward the pit, peels taut skin
clean from plum flesh.

The woman watches his hands,
the pale fruit darkening
wherever he's pushed too hard.

She is thinking *seed,* the hardness
she'll roll on her tongue,
a beginning. One by one,

the man fills the bowl with globes
that glisten. *Translucent,* he thinks.
The woman, now, her cup tilting

empty, sees, for the first time,
the hairline crack
that has begun to split the bowl in half.

At the Station

The blue light was my blues,
and the red light was my mind.
—Robert Johnson

The man, turning, moves away
from the platform. Growing smaller,
he does not say

Come back. She won't. Each
glowing light dims
the farther it moves from reach,

the train pulling clean
out of the station. The woman sits
facing where she's been.

She's chosen her place with care—
each window another eye, another
way of seeing what's back there:

heavy blossoms in afternoon rain
spilling scent and glistening sex.
Everything dripping green.

Blue shade, leaves swollen like desire.
A man motioning *nothing*.
No words. His mind on fire.

Naola Beauty Academy, New Orleans, 1945

Made hair? The girls here
put a press on your head
last two weeks. No naps.

They learning. See the basins?
This where we wash. Yeah,
it's hot. July jam.

Stove always on. Keep the combs
hot. Lee and Ida bumping hair
right now. Best two.

Ida got a natural touch.
Don't burn nobody.
Her own's a righteous mass.

Lee, now she used to sew.
Her fingers steady
from them tiny needles.

She can fix some bad hair.
Look how she lay them waves.
Light, slight, and polite.

Not a one out of place.

Drapery Factory, Gulfport, Mississippi, 1956

She made the trip daily, though
later she would not remember
how far to tell the grandchildren—
Better that way.
She could keep those miles
a secret, and her black face
and black hands, and the pink bottoms
of her black feet
a minor inconvenience.

She does remember the men
she worked for, and that often
she sat side by side
with white women, all of them
bent over, pushing into the hum
of the machines, their right calves
tensed against the pedals.

Her lips tighten speaking
of quitting time when
the colored women filed out slowly
to have their purses checked,
the insides laid open and exposed
by the boss's hand.

        But then she laughs
when she recalls the soiled Kotex
she saved, stuffed into a bag
in her purse, and Adam's look
on one white man's face, his hand
deep in knowledge.

His Hands

His hands will never be large enough.
Not for the woman who sees in his face
the father she can't remember,
or her first husband, the soldier with two wives—
all the men who would only take.
Not large enough to deflect
the sharp edges of her words.

Still he tries to prove himself in work,
his callused hands heaving crates
all day on the docks, his pay twice spent.
He brings home what he can, buckets of crabs
from his morning traps, a few green bananas.

His supper waits in the warming oven,
the kitchen dark, the screens hooked.
He thinks, *make the hands gentle*
as he raps lightly on the back door.
He has never had a key.

Putting her hands to his, she pulls him in,
sets him by the stove. Slowly, she rubs oil
into his cracked palms, drawing out soreness
from the swells, removing splinters, taking
whatever his hands will give.

Self-Employment, 1970

Who to be today? So many choices,
all that natural human hair piled high,
curled and flipped—style after style
perched, each on its Styrofoam head.
Maybe an upsweep, or finger waves
with a ponytail. Not a day passes
that she goes unkempt—
Never know who might stop by—
now that she works at home
pacing the cutting table,
or pumping the stiff pedal
of the bought-on-time Singer.

Most days, she dresses for the weather,
relentless sun, white heat. The one tree
nearest her workroom, a mimosa,
its whimsy of pink puffs cut back
for a child's swing set. And now, grandchildren—
it's come to this—a frenzy of shouts,
the constant *slap* of an old screen door.
At least the radio still swings jazz
just above the noise, and

Ah yes, the window unit—leaky at best.
Sometimes she just stands still, lets
ice water drip onto upturned wrists.
Up under that wig, her head
sweating, hot as an idea.

Early Evening, Frankfort, Kentucky

It is 1965. I am not yet born, only
a fullness beneath the empire waist
of my mother's blue dress.

The ruffles at her neck are waves
of light in my father's eyes. He carries
a slim volume, leather-bound, poems

to read as they walk. The long road
past the college, through town,
rises and falls before them,

the blue hills shimmering at twilight.
The stacks at the distillery exhale,
and my parents breathe evening air

heady and sweet as Kentucky bourbon.
They are young and full of laughter,
the sounds in my mother's throat

rippling down into my blood.
My mother, who will not reach
forty-one, steps into the middle

of a field, lies down among clover
and sweet grass, right here, right now—
dead center of her life.

Cameo

As a child, I would awaken dark mornings
to peer from beneath the bedcovers and watch
my mother dress. She'd perch on a stool
at the cluttered vanity. Under the oil lamp,

golden tubes of lipstick and atomizers glowing
like bottled light. She wore a pale slip, clinging
like water to her back. I'd watch her lean in close,
plucking the small hairs at her brow into points

that aimed down toward the corners of her mouth.
Her dress hung on the closet door as if
after mastectomy, the bodice empty
where her breasts would push against the fabric,

perfume heavy even after dry cleaning—
the warm scent of her body filling the tiny room.
Before she'd move away from the mirror,
my mother would tie on a black velvet ribbon

at the back of her neck, so tight it seemed to hold
her together, the fine bones of her neck in place.
In the front, a cameo pressing into the hollow
of her throat, hard enough to bruise.

Hot Combs

At the junk shop, I find an old pair,
black with grease, the teeth still pungent
as burning hair. One is small,
fine toothed as if for a child. Holding it,
I think of my mother's slender wrist,
the curve of her neck as she leaned
over the stove, her eyes shut as she pulled
the wooden handle and laid flat the wisps
at her temples. The heat in our kitchen
made her glow that morning I watched her
wincing, the hot comb singeing her brow,
sweat glistening above her lips,
her face made strangely beautiful
as only suffering can do.

Family Portrait

Before the picture man comes
Mama and I spend the morning
cleaning the family room. She hums
Motown, doles out chores, a warning—

He has no legs, she says. *Don't stare.*
I'm first to the door when he rings.
My father and uncle lift his chair
onto the porch, arrange his things

near the place his feet would be.
He poses our only portrait—my father
sitting, Mama beside him, and me
in between. I watch him bother

the space for knees, shins, scratching air
as—years later—I'd itch for what's not there.

Mythmaker

We lived by the words
of gods, mythologies

you'd mold our history to.
How many nights, you,

a young father, squint-eyed
from books and lamplight,

weaving lessons into bedtime—
the story of Icarus wanting

to soar, (like me on my swing set)
not heeding a father's words,

his fall likened to mine.
I'd carry his doom to sleep,

and that of Narcissus too,
his watered face floating

beautiful and tragic above
my head. My own face

a mirrored comfort
you'd pull me from. Late,

when my dreams turned
to nightmare, you were there—

Beowulf to slay Grendel
at my door. The blood on your hands

you'd anoint my head with.
You would have me bold, fearless—

these were things you needed
to teach me. Warning and wisdom.

You couldn't have known
how I'd take your words and shape

them in creation, reinvent you
a thousand times, making you

forever young and invincible.
Not like now. Not like now.

Amateur Fighter

—for my father

What's left is the tiny gold glove
hanging from his key chain. But,
before that, he had come to boxing,

as a boy, out of necessity—one more reason
to stay away from home, go late
to that cold house and dinner alone

in the dim kitchen. Perhaps he learned
just to box a stepfather, then turned
that anger into a prize at the Halifax gym.

Later, in New Orleans, there were the books
he couldn't stop reading. A scholar, his eyes
weakening. Fighting, then, a way to live

dangerously. He'd leave his front tooth out
for pictures so that I might understand
living meant suffering, loss. Really living

meant taking risks, so he swallowed
a cockroach in a bar on a dare, dreamt
of being a bullfighter. And at the gym

on Tchoupitoulas Street, he trained
his fists to pound into a bag
the fury contained in his gentle hands.

The red headgear, hiding his face,
could make me think he was someone else,
that my father was somewhere else, not here

holding his body up to pain.

Flounder

Here, she said, *put this on your head.*
She handed me a hat.
You 'bout as white as your dad,
and you gone stay like that.

Aunt Sugar rolled her nylons down
around each bony ankle,
and I rolled down my white knee socks
letting my thin legs dangle,

circling them just above water
and silver backs of minnows
flitting here then there between
the sun spots and the shadows.

This is how you hold the pole
to cast the line out straight.
Now put that worm on your hook,
throw it out and wait.

She sat spitting tobacco juice
into a coffee cup.
Hunkered down when she felt the bite,
jerked the pole straight up

reeling and tugging hard at the fish
that wriggled and tried to fight back.
A flounder, she said, *and you can tell*
'cause one of its sides is black.

The other side is white, she said.
It landed with a thump.
I stood there watching that fish flip-flop,
switch sides with every jump.

White Lies

The lies I could tell,
when I was growing up
light-bright, near-white,
high-yellow, red-boned
in a black place,
were just white lies.

I could easily tell the white folks
that we lived uptown,
not in that pink and green
shanty-fied shotgun section
along the tracks. I could act
like my homemade dresses
came straight out the window
of Maison Blanche. I could even
keep quiet, quiet as kept,
like the time a white girl said
(squeezing my hand), *Now
we have three of us in this class.*

But I paid for it every time
Mama found out.
She laid her hands on me,
then washed out my mouth
with Ivory soap. *This
is to purify,* she said,
and cleanse your lying tongue.
Believing her, I swallowed suds
thinking they'd work
from the inside out.

Microscope

In sixth grade, science was a puzzle
of shifting shapes—Africa, Europe,
and the Americas—fitting together
as we'd float wooden plates over
a background of blue. Small discoveries,
magnetic push and pull, dull rocks
breaking open to colored gemstone,
fool's gold, and stars—already dead
we were told—lighting the planetarium roof.

At home I'd find science in swampy ditches
teeming life—small worlds to swirl and multiply
in my petri dish—or an onion skin translucent
as dragonfly wings. In the *World Book
Encyclopedia 1966,* bought for the year
I was born, I looked for *Rays of Light*
and found, instead, *Races of Man*:
skull measurements and body equations,
chin to forehead, femur to tibia. Pictures
detailing *Caucasoid, Negroid, Mongoloid.*
Hair texture, eye shape, color. Each image
a template for measure, mismeasure.

I collected hair from everybody at home,
and offered up samples at school—my own,
straight and shiny, first; then my brother's
tight curls waiting in a plastic dish.
I've got it, but it's just a tad bit dirty,
the teacher said focusing, his face pressed

against the eyepiece, showing me how
anything—fool's gold, a dead star, my hair,
all of science, glittering and out of reach—
up close could lose its luster.

Saturday Matinee

When I first see *Imitation of Life,*
the 1959 version with Lana Turner
and Sandra Dee, I already know the story
has a mixed girl in it—someone like me,
a character I can shape my life to.
It begins with a still of blue satin
upon which diamonds fall, slowly at first,
and then faster, crowding my television
with rays of light, a sparkling world.

In my room I'm a Hollywood starlet
stretched across my bed, beneath
a gold and antique white canopy,
heavy swags cut from fringed brocade
and pieced together—all remnants
of my grandmother's last job.
Down the hall, my mother whispers
resistance, my stepfather's voice louder
than the static of an old seventy-eight.

Lana Turner glides on screen,
the camera finding her in glowing white,
golden-haired among the crowd.
She is not like my mother, or
the mixed girl's mother—that tired black maid
she hires—and I can see why the mixed girl
wants her, instead, a mother always smiling
from a fifties magazine. She doesn't want
the run-down mama, her blues—

dark circles around the eyes,
that weary step and *hush-baby* tone.
My gold room is another world.
I turn the volume up, over the dull smack,
the stumbling for balance, the clutter of voices
in the next room. I'll be Sandra Dee,
and Lana Turner, my mother—our lives
an empty screen, pale blue, diamonds falling
until it's all covered up.

IV

History Lesson

I am four in this photograph, standing
on a wide strip of Mississippi beach,
my hands on the flowered hips

of a bright bikini. My toes dig in,
curl around wet sand. The sun cuts
the rippling Gulf in flashes with each

tidal rush. Minnows dart at my feet
glinting like switchblades. I am alone
except for my grandmother, other side

of the camera, telling me how to pose.
It is 1970, two years after they opened
the rest of this beach to us,

forty years since the photograph
where she stood on a narrow plot
of sand marked *colored*, smiling,

her hands on the flowered hips
of a cotton meal-sack dress.

Saturday Drive

—for my mother

Saturdays, Uncle Son drives slow;
that '59, white-walled, cash-money
Cadillac—neighborhood El Dog—creeping
down Highway 49 past the curb market
liquor store car wash barbershop.

Beside him, the girl folds lace gloves
in her lap and smoothes the taped-down edges
of a cigar box turned coin bank, a single slit
in the top just big enough to look through
and see nothing but dark.

A right turn on I-90 and Son Dixon
speeds up, heading West, the green Gulf
on one side, the white-columned mansions
of folks with names like ours—Dixon, Dedeaux,
and Davis—on the other. Flip side.

On the last bridge outside New Orleans
she measures the air's heady scents—leather,
shave tonic, tobacco—each one a way to recall
this drive, the long reflection in flat water.
Noon sun overhead, a sheet of black glass below.

At the downtown shop Uncle Son buys
every record just pressed—new music
for his Owl Club jukebox—the promise
to a young girl that she'll have each one
soon, those black discs unscratched,

still shiny enough to see her face in.

Accounting

Nights too warm for TV
we're flung outdoors to the porch,
citronella candles scenting the space
between us, our faces aglow
in gold light. She crowds the card table
with coin banks, an abacus,
five and ten dollar rolling paper,
our tidy ledger.

I count, line the coins in neat rows,
the abacus clicking out our worth,
how much we can save, stack up
against the seasons—winter coming,
her tightly braided hair turning white;
her hands quick, filling the paper casings
like homemade sausage.

There's money in the bank downtown,
but this we'll keep at home
buried in jars beneath the house,
the crawl space filling up, packed solid
as any foundation.

Gathering

—for Sugar

Through tall grass, heavy
from rain, my aunt and I wade
into cool, fruit trees.

Near us, dragonflies
light on the clothesline, each touch
rippling to the next.

Green-black beetles swarm
the fruit, wings droning motion,
wet figs glistening.

We sigh, click our tongues,
our fingers reaching in, then
plucking what is left.

Under-ripe figs, green,
hard as jewels—these we save,
hold in deep white bowls.

She puts them to light
on the windowsill, tells me
to *wait, learn patience.*

I touch them each day,
watch them turn gold, grow sweet,
and give sweetness back.

I begin to see
our lives are like this—we take
what we need of light.

We glisten, preserve
handpicked days in memory,
our minds' dark pantry.

Give and Take

I come here once a month to dig
my fingers into your head, grease
your scalp, put you in plaits for ease—
old woman, I remember

the photograph you used to pull out;
Chicago, 1957, lab coat on,
you are bent over test tubes
adding substance to substance.

I imagine you before the flame
taking something out, distilling
light from volatile darkness,
and handing it over. You had begun

to hand over everything else, piece
by piece, each time I visited.
The trinket shelf grew empty
in the corner. I walked away

with the tiny mortar and pestle,
the cracked figurine, the nativity
under glass. Then we took
what you chose not to give:

all the knives in the house,
your hot plate and stove. Still,
you cooked on the radiator, forgot,
and singed your matted wig.

Now your lab coat is an open frock,
easy for the Dixie White House staff
who wipe and clean your bony back.
And every time I see you,

you're gathering stuff up, stashing it
in your pockets, in the elastic
waist of your panties, even
the corners of your mouth.

Housekeeping

We mourn the broken things, chair legs
wrenched from their seats, chipped plates,
the threadbare clothes. We work the magic
of glue, drive the nails, mend the holes.
We save what we can, melt small pieces
of soap, gather fallen pecans, keep neck bones
for soup. Beating rugs against the house,
we watch dust, lit like stars, spreading
across the yard. Late afternoon, we draw
the blinds to cool the rooms, drive the bugs
out. My mother irons, singing, lost in reverie.
I mark the pages of a mail-order catalog,
listen for passing cars. All day we watch
for the mail, some news from a distant place.

Picture Gallery

In a tight corner of the house, we'd kept
the light-up portraits of Kennedy and King,
side by side, long after the bulbs burned out—

cords tangling on the floor, and the patina
of rust slowly taking the filigreed frames.

Then, my grandmother wanted more *Art*—
something beautiful to look at, she said.
At the fabric store she bought bolts of cloth

printed with natural scenes—far-off views
of mountains, owls on snowy boughs.

I donated the scenic backdrop that came
with a model horse—a yellowed vista
of wheat fields, a wagon, and one long road.

Back home, we gathered pinecones
and branches, staples and glue, then hung

the fabric, big as windows, in the dark
hallway. The fresh boughs we stapled on
stuck out in relief. We breathed green air,

and the owls—instead—peered in at us,
our lives suddenly beautiful, then.

Collection Day

Saturday morning, Motown
forty-fives and thick seventy-eights
on the phonograph, window fans
turning light into our rooms,
we clean house to a spiral groove,
sorting through our dailiness—
washtubs of boiled-white linens,
lima beans soaking, green as luck,
trash heaped out back for burning—
everything we can't keep,
make new with thread or glue.

Beside the stove, a picture calendar
of the seasons, daily scripture,
compliments of the Everlast Interment
Company, one day each month marked
in red—PREMIUM DUE—collection visit
from the insurance man, his black suits
worn to a shine. In our living room
he'll pull out photos of our tiny plot,
show us the slight eastward slope,
all the flowers in bloom now, how neat
the shrubs are trimmed, and *See here,
the trees we planted are coming up fine.*

We look out for him all day, listen
for the turn-stop of wheels
and rocks crunching underfoot.
Mama leafs through the Bible
for our payment card—June 1969,
the month he'll stamp PAID

in bright green letters, putting us
one step closer to what we'll own,
something to last: patch of earth,
view of sky.

Carpenter Bee

All winter long I have passed
beneath her nest—a hole no bigger
than the tip of my thumb.

Last year, before I was here,
she burrowed into the wood
framing my porch, drilled a network

of tunnels, her round body sturdy
for the work of building. Torpid
the cold months, she now pulls herself

out into the first warm days of spring
to tread the air outside my screen door,
floating in pure sunlight, humming

against a backdrop of green. She too
must smell the wisteria, see
—with her hundreds of eyes—purple

blossoms lacing the trees. Flower-
hopping, she draws invisible lines,
the geometry of her flight. Drunk

on nectar, she can still find her way
back; though now, she must be
confused, disoriented, doubting even

her own homing instinct—this beeline,
now, to nowhere. Today, the workmen
have come, plugged the hole—her threshold—

covered it with thick white paint, a scent
acrid and unfamiliar. She keeps hovering,
buzzing around the spot. Watching her,

I think of what I've left behind, returned to,
only to find everything changed, nothing but
my memory intact—like her eggs, still inside,

each in its separate cell—snug, ordered, certain.

Limen

All day I've listened to the industry
of a single woodpecker, worrying the catalpa tree
just outside my window. Hard at his task,

his body is a hinge, a door knocker
to the cluttered house of memory in which
I can almost see my mother's face.

She is there, again, beyond the tree,
its slender pods and heart-shaped leaves,
hanging wet sheets on the line—each one

a thin white screen between us. So insistent
is this woodpecker, I'm sure he must be
looking for something else—not simply

the beetles and grubs inside, but some other gift
the tree might hold. All day he's been at work,
tireless, making the green hearts flutter.

Natasha Trethewey was born in Gulfport, Mississippi, in 1966. She has received fellowships from the Alabama State Council on the Arts and the National Endowment for the Arts and won the Grolier Poetry Prize. Her poems have appeared in the *Best American Poetry 2000,* the *American Poetry Review,* the *Gettysburg Review, New England Review,* and the *Southern Review,* among other magazines and anthologies. She is a member of the Dark Room Collective and teaches English at Auburn University in Alabama. She currently holds a Bunting Fellowship in Cambridge, Massachusetts.

About Cave Canem

Cave Canem was founded in 1996 by poets Toi Derricotte and Cornelius Eady to promote the artistic development of African American poets. Cave Canem's workshops offer Black poets an opportunity to work together in a welcoming atmosphere and to study with accomplished African American poets and teachers. It has grown into a national community and a home for the rich diversity of Black poetry.

The Cave Canem Poetry Prize is an annual award for the best first collection of poems submitted by an African American poet, selected for publication by an accomplished writer. *Domestic Work* is the first winner of the Cave Canem Poetry Prize, selected by former United States Poet Laureate Rita Dove.

This book was designed by Wendy Holdman. It is set in Calisto type by Stanton Publication Services, Inc., and manufactured by Bang Printing on acid-free paper.

Graywolf Press is a not-for-profit, independent press. The books we publish include poetry, literary fiction, and cultural criticism. We are less interested in best-sellers than in talented writers who display a freshness of voice coupled with a distinct vision. We believe these are the very qualities essential to shape a vital and diverse culture.

Thankfully, many of our readers feel the same way. They have shown this through their desire to buy books by Graywolf writers; they have told us this themselves through their e-mail notes and at author events; and they have reinforced their commitment by contributing financial support, in small amounts and in large amounts, and joining the "Friends of Graywolf."

If you enjoyed this book and wish to learn more about Graywolf Press, we invite you to ask your bookseller or librarian about further Graywolf titles; or to contact us for a free catalog; or to visit our award-winning web site that features information about our forthcoming books.

We would also like to invite you to consider joining the hundreds of individuals who are already "Friends of Graywolf" by contributing to our membership program. Individual donations of any size are significant to us: they tell us that you believe that the kind of publishing we do *matters*. Our web site gives you many more details about the benefits you will enjoy as a "Friend of Graywolf"; but if you do not have online access, we urge you to contact us for a copy of our membership brochure.

www.graywolfpress.org

Graywolf Press
2402 University Avenue, Suite 203
Saint Paul, MN 55114
Phone: (651) 641-0077
Fax: (651) 641-0036
E-mail: wolves@graywolfpress.org

Graywolf Press is dedicated to the creation and promotion of thoughtful and imaginative contemporary literature essential to a vital and diverse culture. For further information, visit us online at: www.graywolfpress.org.

Other Graywolf titles you might enjoy are:

Tug by G.E. Patterson
Red Signature by Mary Leader
One Crossed Out by Fanny Howe
Except by Nature by Sandra Alcosser
Full Moon Boat by Fred Marchant
By Herself: Women Reclaim Poetry, edited by Molly McQuade